God is...

How do we know about God? We can see the wonderful world that God has made and we can read about God in the Bible. That's why it's so exciting to learn to read! You're learning that those squiggles on the page we call letters make sounds, and that you can blend those sounds together to read words. The Bible is a big book with a great many words. It's actually a collection of books written by different people over many years. The remarkable thing is that these books all tell part of the same story – the story of how much God loves us.

Let's see what the Bible says about God.

You read the **big print** and I'll read the small print.

God is.

The man in this Bible story is called Moses. God spoke to him from a burning bush. Moses wanted to know God's name and God simply said, **"I AM WHO I AM."** (Exodus 3:13-14)

God is big. I am not.

Have you ever looked up at the sky at night-time and felt rather small? There are songs in the Bible called Psalms which tell us a lot about God. Psalm 8 says, **"When I look at the night sky and see the work of your fingers – the moon and the stars you set in place – what are people that you should think about them, mere mortals that you should care for them?"** (Psalm 8:3-4)

God is up, up, up.

We think of God being up in the heavens, greater than anything or anyone else. Psalm 113 says, **"Who can be compared with the LORD our God, who is enthroned on high?"** (Psalm 113:5)

But God is in us.

The man in this Bible story is called Paul. He is telling the people of Athens about God. He tells them that God is very close to us, and that **"... in him we live and move and exist..."** (Acts 17:27-28).

God is a rock.

We really mean God is *like* a rock, steady and dependable. God won't let us down and God keeps us safe. Psalm 18 says, **"... my God is my rock, in whom I find protection..."** (Psalm 18:2).

God can help us.

It's good to pray to God and ask for help. Psalm 121 says, **"My help comes from the LORD, who made heaven and earth!"** (Psalm 121:2)

I can rest in God. God will not end.

It's good to know that God is big and everywhere, yet so close to us. God loves us very much. Psalm 4:8 says, **"In peace I will lie down and sleep, for you alone, O LORD, will keep me safe."**